W9-BDN-561

J583.32 SE49
Selsam, Millicent Ellis.
Peanut

Mid-Continent Public Library
15616 East US Highway 24
Independence, MO 64050

AWARD(S) WON

Notable Children's Books   1969

THIS BOOK WITHDRAWN FROM
THE RECORDS OF THE

DEC 3 1 2019

MID-CONTINENT PUBLIC LIBRARY

PEANUT

MID-CONTINENT PUBLIC LIBRARY

J583.32   Se49
Selsam, Millicent E.
Peanut   10.95

PEANUT

MILLICENT E. SELSAM
Photographs by JEROME WEXLER

William Morrow and Company
New York

Mid-Continent Public Library
15616 East US Highway 24
Independence, MO 64050

MID-CONTINENT PUBLIC LIBRARY

3 0000 12745914 1

Copyright © 1969 by Millicent E. Selsam
All rights reserved. No part of this book may be reproduced or utilized
in any form or by any means, electronic or mechanical, including photocopying, recording
or by any information storage and retrieval system,
without permission in writing from the Publisher. Inquiries should be addressed to
William Morrow and Company, Inc., 105 Madison Ave.,
New York, N.Y. 10016.
Printed in the United States of America
Library of Congress Catalog Card Number 70–81886
Design by Cynthia Basil

By the Same Author

ANIMALS AS PARENTS
THE COURTSHIP OF ANIMALS
HOW ANIMALS LIVE TOGETHER
HOW ANIMALS TELL TIME
HOW TO GROW HOUSE PLANTS
THE LANGUAGE OF ANIMALS
MAPLE TREE
MICROBES AT WORK
MILKWEED
PLANTS THAT HEAL
PLANTS THAT MOVE
THE PLANTS WE EAT
PLAY WITH PLANTS
PLAY WITH SEEDS
PLAY WITH TREES
UNDERWATER ZOOS

The author and photographer thank
Dr. Howard S. Irwin,
Head Curator
of the New York Botanical Gardens
for checking the text
and photographs of this book.

ACKNOWLEDGMENTS FOR PHOTOGRAPHS
Alabama and Georgia Peanut Growers, 8, 9 right, 41
American Museum of Natural History, 45 right
Columbia University, Department of Anthropology, 45 left
New York Public Library, Schomburg Collection, 11 right
United States Department of Agriculture, 10, 42, 43

One more peanut is never enough.

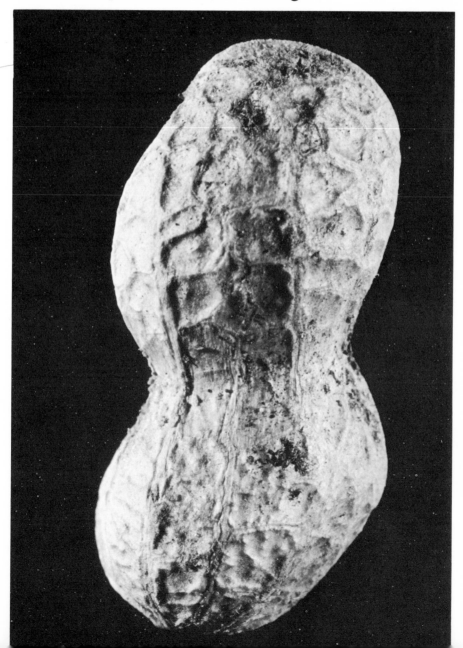

We eat tons of peanuts every year.
Peanuts are a good food.
One pound has more food value
than a pound of beef has.

Lots of peanuts are made
into peanut butter.
Lots of peanuts are used to make
peanut candy and peanut cookies.

Peanut oil is pressed from peanuts.
It is used for cooking oil,
for salad oil, and to make oleomargarine.
It is also used to make
soap, face powder, and shampoo.

JARS OF PEANUT OIL BEING CAPPED

After the oil is removed from peanuts,
the solid part that is left is used to feed cattle and pigs.
Or the solids may be used to make synthetic fibers.
Even peanut shells are used. They become part
of plastics, wallboard, linoleum, and polishes.

At the beginning of this century
a famous American scientist,
George Washington Carver,
developed three hundred ways
to use the peanut plant.

SYNTHETIC
FIBER

What is the peanut plant like?
You can plant a peanut and find out.
But don't try to plant a roasted peanut.
It won't grow, because it is all dried out inside.
Plant a fresh, unroasted peanut,
the kind you buy in a seed store.
It will start to grow faster
if you soak the peanut overnight first.

This picture shows a soaked peanut split open.
Notice the baby plant, called the embryo,
attached to one of the peanut halves.
The halves of the peanut are called seed leaves
and are full of stored food.
The embryo uses this food as it grows.

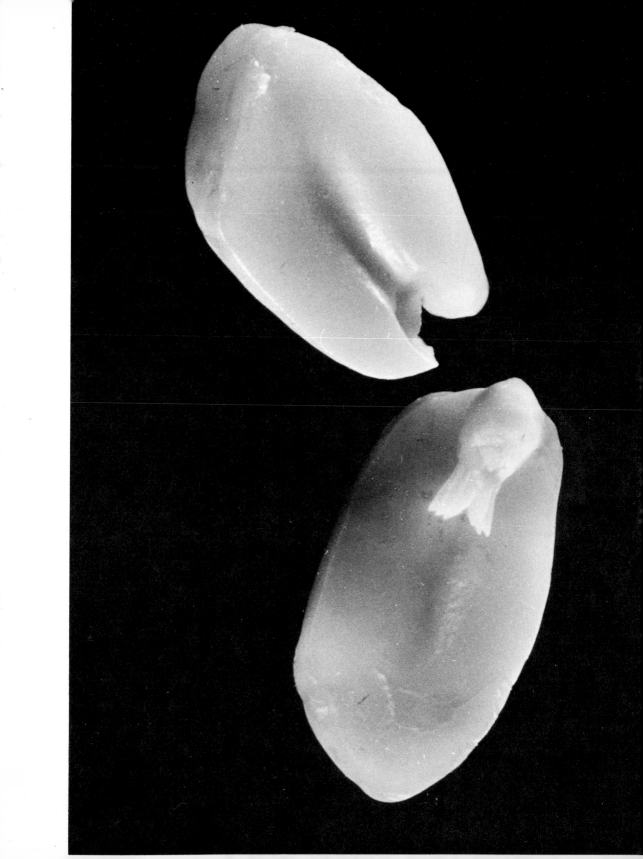

The soaked peanuts have been placed
between wet paper and the glass.
In this way you can see what happens.

The embryo is growing.
The part that comes out first
grows into the root.

Side roots form.

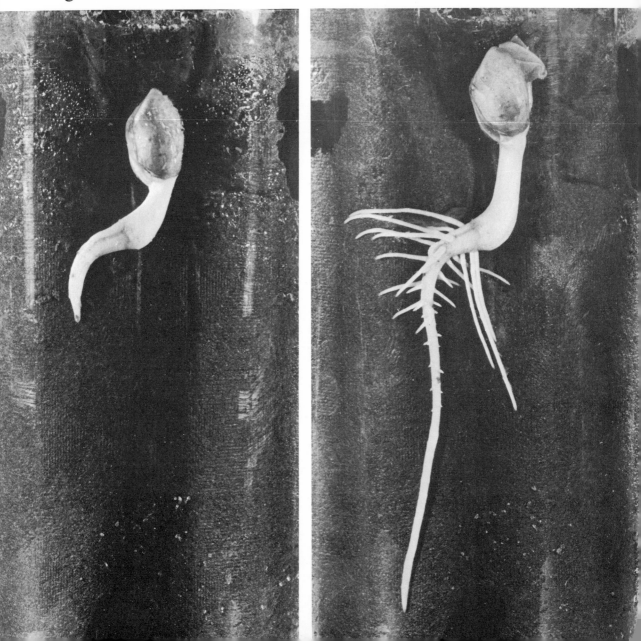

Then the young stem and leaves
come out from between the seed leaves.

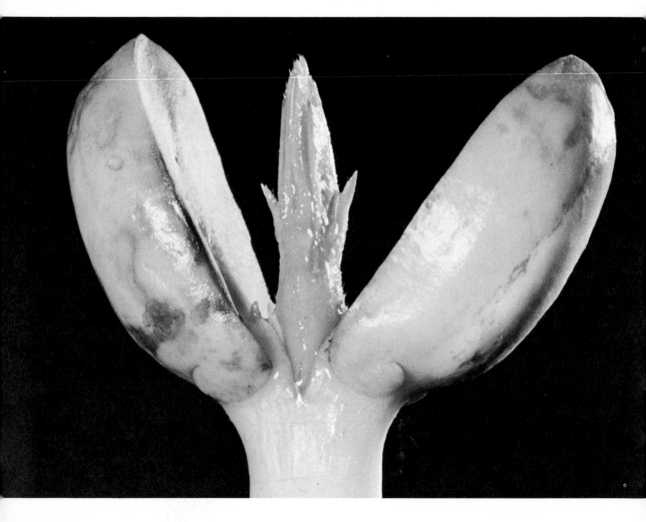

Here you can see the first real leaves.

The peanut can grow inside the shell too.
This one is growing into the ground.

Now the leaves are showing above the ground.

The peanut plant grows bigger and bigger.

The leaves of the peanut plant
are open during the day.

At night they fold up
into a "sleeping" position.

Soon small yellow flowers appear.
They are low on the plant.

Flower buds open at sunrise.
This yellow flower is different from a simple flower.
It looks like the flower of a sweet pea.

A simple flower
like this lily
has petals arranged in a circle
around a center.

But the peanut flower
has one large petal in back,
two side petals,
and two small petals
joined together in front.

The most important parts in any flower
are the stamens and pistils.
They are the organs necessary for seed making.
Without them, the peanut plant cannot make peanuts.

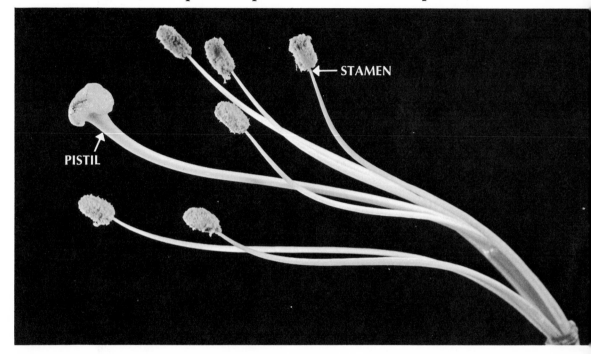

Usually the stamens and pistil
are in the center of the flower.
In this picture of a lily the petals have been removed.
You can see the stamens around a pistil in the center.
Sometimes there are many pistils.

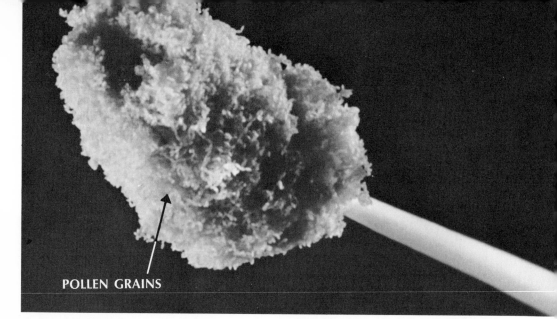

POLLEN GRAINS

The stamens have little bags of pollen grains at the top.
The grains look like yellow dust.
Sometimes pollen is brown or purple.
The pistil is made up of a top part, called the stigma,
connected by a stalk to a bottom part, called the ovary.
The stigma is sticky and catches the pollen.

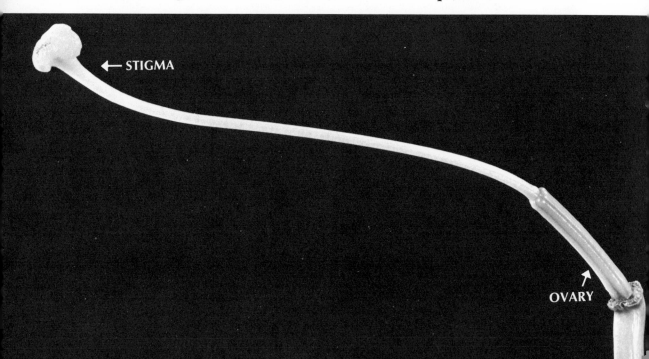

← STIGMA

OVARY

Inside the ovary are ovules, or seeds-to-be.
They become seeds when they are fertilized, or joined,
by the contents of a pollen grain.

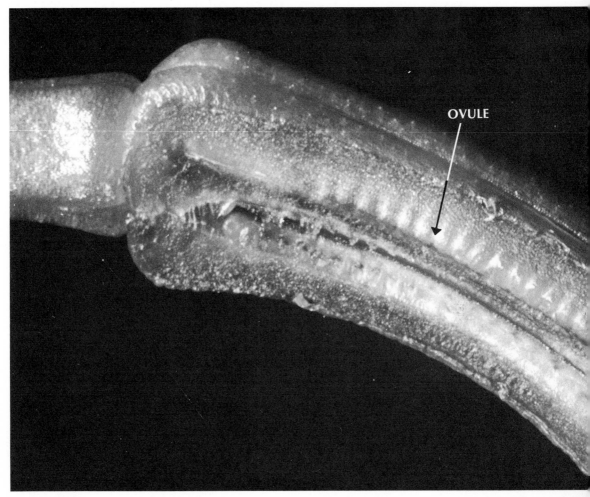

OVULE

But where are
the stamens and pistil
in the peanut flower?
They are hidden inside
the two small joined front petals.
These two joined petals look
like a boat with a round bottom.
One of the stamens
is sticking up.

Here the flower is open, and you can see
the stamens and the top of the pistil (stigma).

The ovary is in a peculiar place in the peanut flower.
In the lily, as in most simple flowers,
the ovary can be found
where the petals of a flower join together
or just underneath that point.

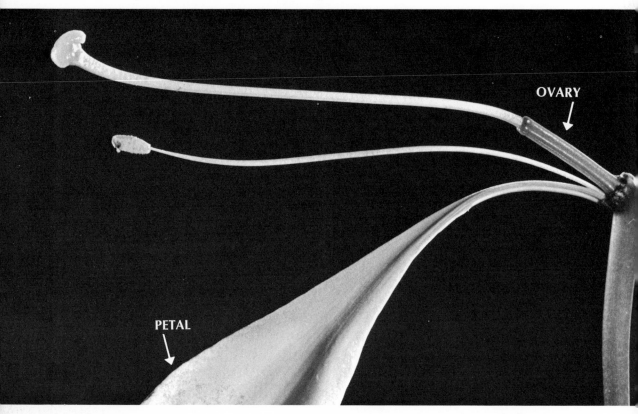

OVARY

PETAL

But the petals of the peanut flower
are at the top of a long tube,
and the ovary is all the way down at the bottom of it. ▶

Inside this long tube
there is a stalk
that connects the stigma
to the ovary
at the bottom.

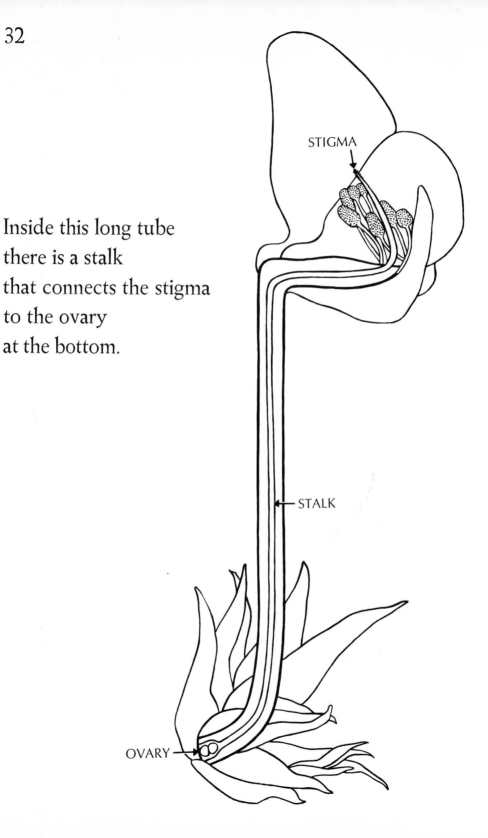

STIGMA

STALK

OVARY

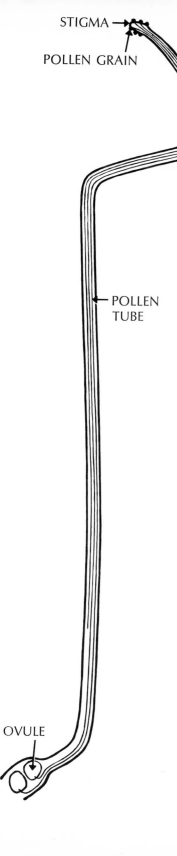

STIGMA

POLLEN GRAIN

POLLEN
TUBE

OVULE

Even before
the peanut flower
opens in the morning,
the stamens slit open
and pollen sifts out
onto the stigma
in the same flower.
This process is called
self-pollination.
Then the pollen puts out
its own tube,
which grows down the long stalk
of the pistil
until it reaches the ovary.
This growth takes
less than four hours.
The contents
of each pollen tube
join with each ovule.
Now the ovules
are fertilized
and can change into seeds.

After pollination
the flower withers.
There is
one withered flower
and one flower bud
in this picture.

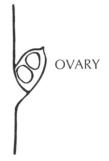 OVARY

All the parts
above the ovary
of the withered flower
fall off now.

The ovary
does not change much
for a few days.
Then it starts to grow
in a most unusual way.
Instead of staying
in one place
and getting bigger,
the way most ovaries do,
it turns down and grows
toward the earth.
You can see
one ovary growing
in this picture.
Most people call it a *peg*,
when it starts
to grow downward.

PEG

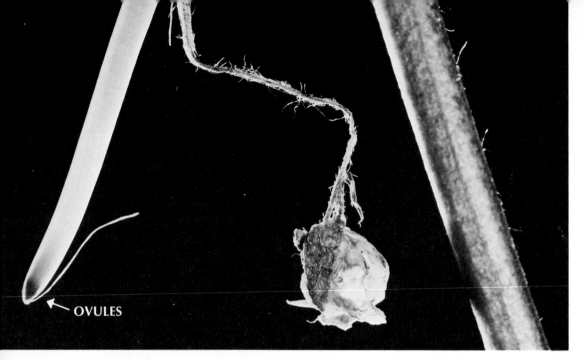

OVULES

Here you can see the dark ovules
at the very bottom of the peg.

The pegs continue to grow down into the soil
until they are one to three inches deep.

Then the tips of the pegs
get bigger and turn sideways.
This picture of a plant dug out of the ground
shows what the pegs look like at this stage.

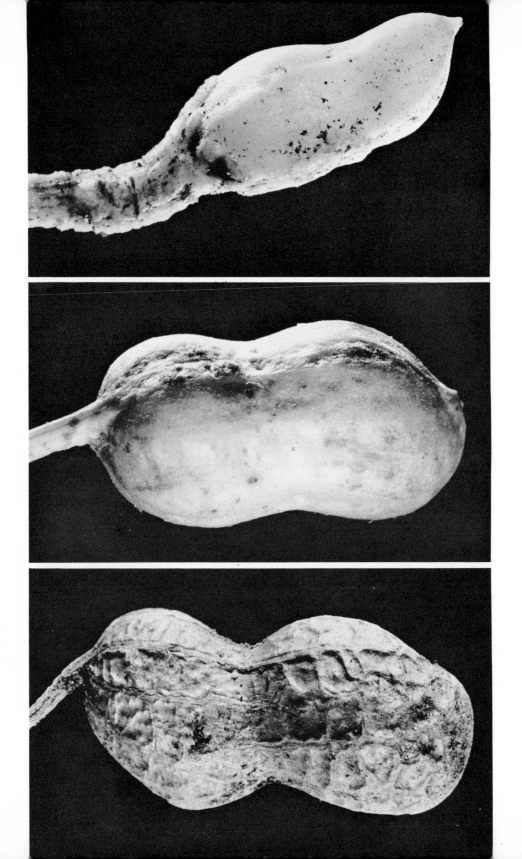

The tip of each peg becomes a peanut
with a papery shell around it. Inside it are the seeds.
The peanut is not really a nut, but a pod
like a bean pod that contains two beans.
Peanut plants are related to pea and bean plants.

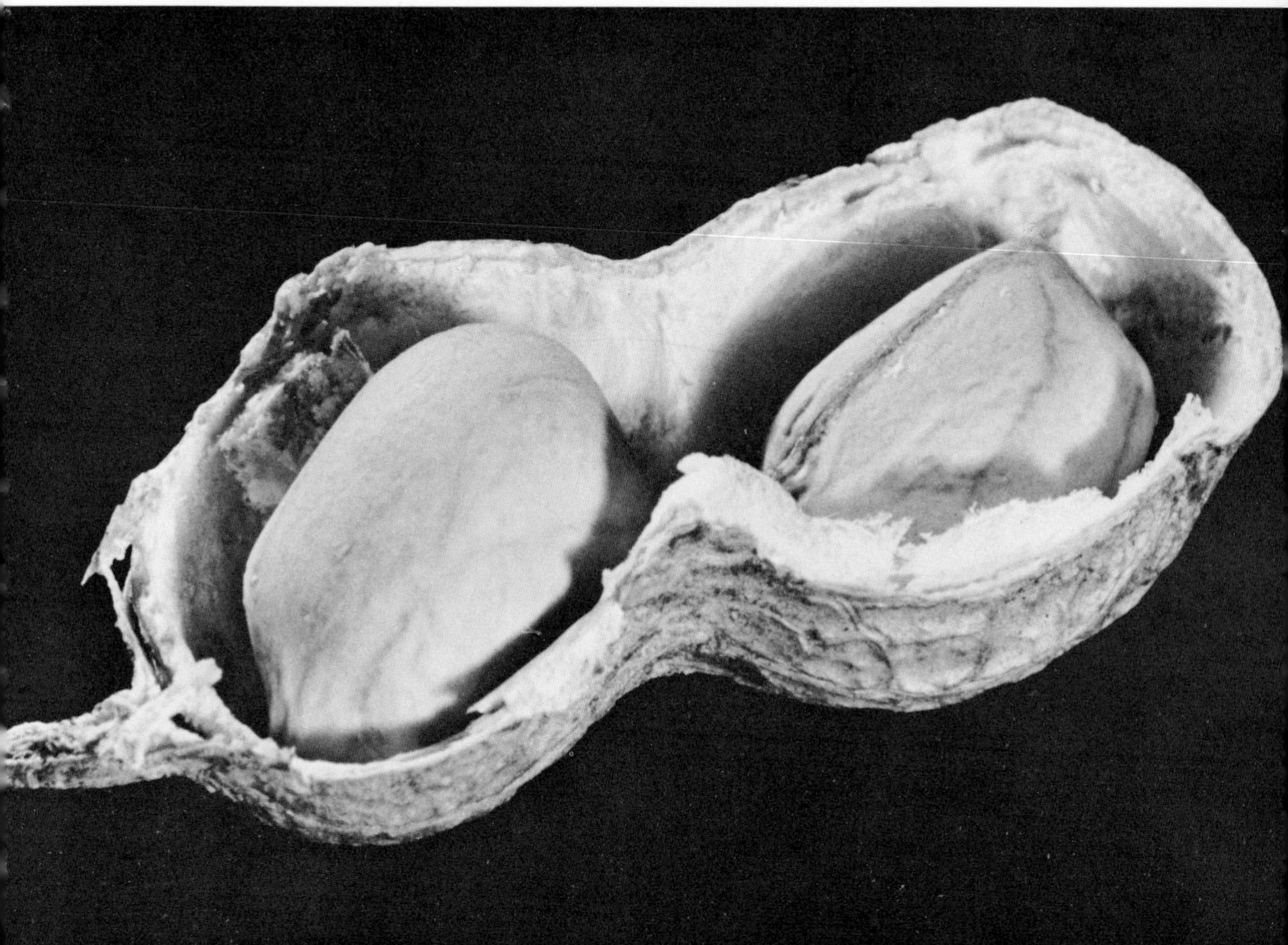

A pod is a fruit, because it contains seeds.
But the peanut fruit is a strange one,
for it grows under the ground.

Here is a peanut farm.
The plants have to be dug up
when the nuts are ripe.

This digger-shaker machine lifts the plants
from under the ground and places them in rows.
After a few days the plants,
spread out on the ground,
are dry enough for the next operation.

This combine picks the nuts off the vines.
Then the peanuts are dried.
The rest of the plant is left on the field.
It is either dug into the ground
or fed to cattle and pigs.

The peanut plant has traveled all over the world
from its home in South America.
At first the experts thought
it had come from Asia and Africa,
because there were so many peanuts growing there.
But then tombs more than fifteen hundred years old
were opened in Peru, and next to the mummies were jars,
some of which had peanut designs on them.

Portuguese slave traders probably took
peanuts from South America to Africa.
Other explorers carried the plant to Asia.
In a short time the peanut was growing
throughout the warm countries of the world
and still is today.

The Spanish peanut, a small type of peanut plant,
is the one photographed in this book.

ABOUT THE AUTHOR

Millicent E. Selsam's career has been closely connected with biology and botany. She majored in biology and was graduated *magna cum laude* with a B.A. degree from Brooklyn College. At Columbia she received her M.A. in the Department of Botany, and since then has passed all course requirements and a comprehensive examination for a Ph.D., also at Columbia. After teaching biology for ten years in the New York City high schools, she has devoted herself to writing science books for children.

Mrs. Selsam and her husband live in New York City and spend their summers on Fire Island, New York.

ABOUT THE PHOTOGRAPHER

Jerome Wexler was born in New York City, where he attended Pratt Institute. Later he studied at the University of Connecticut. His interest in photography started when he was in the ninth grade. After service in World War II, he worked for the State Department in Europe as a photographer. Returning to the United States, he specialized in photographing advanced farming techniques, and the pictures he made have been published throughout the world. When he became interested in nature photography some five years ago, he could not find equipment suited to his needs, so he designed and built his own with which he can photograph living plants and insects ten times their life size.

Mr. Wexler lives, with his wife and two children, in Yalesville, Connecticut.

MID-CONTINENT PUBLIC LIBRARY